FROM COCAINE TO CHRIST

A STORY OF REDEMPTION, RECONCILIATION AND RECOVERY

BRIAN O. MOHIKA

KINGDOM PRINTS

This book is copyrighted by Kingdom Prints

Copyright © 2019.

All rights reserved.

ISBN-13: 978-1-58502-045-4

ISBN-10: 1-58502-045-1

No part of this publication may be reproduced, stored in a retrieval system or transmitted in any way by any means, electronic, mechanical, photocopy, recording, or otherwise, without the prior permission of the author except as provided by USA copyright law.

Cover designed by Jose Aljovin, http://www.josealjovin.com/

Edited by Lisa Thompson at www.writebylisa.com. You can email Lisa at writebylisa@gmail.com.

All Scripture is taken from the New King James Version®. Copyright © 1982 by Thomas Nelson. Used by permission. All rights reserved.

FOREWORD

Brian O. Mohika first came to New Life Christian Assembly of God, Haverhill, Ma in 2010. When we first met, as most pastors usually are, I was very curious about this energetic and charismatic young man that graced our fellowship. He definitely had a personality that gabbed my attention! The next months and years were filled with opportunities to come to know him, to know his world, and to know his struggles. Pastoring certainly has its challenges, even as is my case, after years and years of experience. But with every person there is a story, and with every story there are many roads to travel and mountains to climb and valleys to crawl out of. May I say, pastoring Brian Mohika has been quite a ride! And it has been a very worthwhile endeavor. Sometimes pastors do not have opportunities to see the results of

FOREWORD

their ministry nor the results of God's work in people's lives due to relocation, either physically (for whatever reason), or spiritually, or both. I have had the privilege of walking step by step with Brian for many years now, and have experienced how the Lord saved him, delivered him, shaped him, uses him, and continues to hone in on his strengths, weaknesses, and talents. The Lord is still molding Brian into the man of God He desires him to become, for there are many new endeavors that must be realized in and through his life. For me, this is a very rewarding and exhilarating experience, and I would not trade in the opportunity for anything!

Do you believe that God, the creator of the universe, still speaks today? Do you ever wonder if there is a real hope in the world that could take a person, any person, good or bad, and pour into that soul, life, hope and purpose? Do you think that God cares about those that struggle in life, even those that self-defiantly choose their own path and wind up worse than before? I am here to tell you, God does speak and He does care. He cared so much that "... He gave His only begotten Son, that whoever believes in Him should not perish but have everlasting life" John 3:16 (NKJV.) However, reading the Bible is one thing, and seeing it lived out in real life is quite another.

"From Cocaine To Christ" is a literal telling of one

man's story how God reached down and plucked him out of the fire and destruction of this life and lovingly gave him a new one. It is a gritty tale of one's journey from a life of abuse, self-doubt, drug and alcohol addiction, chaos, pride and self-centeredness to a life of surrender, to God, to family, to church. This is a story of how God has taken an injured soul, and turned him around to be a faithful man, husband, and father to his children. If you, or someone you know is curious about how God operates on ground zero, or perhaps is having his or her own rough go of life, this book is definitely for you. From a difficult family background, from being caught up in the legal system, from marital failure, from deep addictions and self medications, God has brought to Brian deliverance, healing, new beginnings, and victories! Now a faithful family man, a leader in his local church, a prominent person in the medical field, a well-respected inventor, and well on his way to ministerial credentials, Brian's story is one of hope and trust in a living and faithful God "that shows no partiality" (see Acts 10:34, NKJV), but rather steadfastly loves and pours into each and every person He created.

Brian takes you on his journey. Granted, everyone's story is unique, and Brian's is just that. It is custom-made by God Himself. Only God would know what it would take to reach Brian, to get and to keep his focus and attention. We see a young man with so much potential, yet bruised and scattered in a million directions. We see how God constrains Brian, and sets him on the proper course where his gifts, which are many, could be used for the betterment of humanity, and for the furtherance of the Gospel. It is a modern-day example of God at work, a man willing to trust, and a life yielded to the Almighty. Brian's story brings to the forefront the scripture found in Ephesians 2:10, "For we are His workmanship, created in Christ Jesus for good works, which God prepared beforehand that we should walk in them" (NKJV.) Brian's relationship with Christ has opened the door of personal salvation, fulfillment, creativity, and purpose. This story is designed to remind the reader that this experience is available for all that would dare trust God with their past, present and future.

I am excited about this book! I am excited about Brian O. Mohika! This work is a beginning, not an end. This is what I would call, the "first chapter" of a life being lived for God. I am certain there will be more chapters of Brian's life in the years that follow. When I first met that energetic and charismatic young man, I knew there was tremendous potential there. Granted, Brian's big and loving personality will touch many souls with his story. Beneath that story is the backstory of redemption from a God that looked past his failures and shortcomings, and unleashed the power and beauty that He had already placed within.

One last thought. Speaking of the "backstory", there certainly is another backstory to Brian's story. And that is, never underestimate the power of a praying mom! For years his mom, Ms. Paulina Lopez, prayed and prayed and often spoke words of faith and encouragement into her son's heart, mind and spirit. Perhaps this is a primary takeaway from the book: prayer matters! May we take this to heart and keep in prayer before Almighty God all the things that concern us, and may we have a profound faith that our God is able to personalize Himself to each one of us. The Lord did it for Brian, and He will do it for you.

Rev Rick Amendola
New Life Christian Assembly of God
Haverhill, MA

INTRODUCTION

THE DOUBLE LIFE I lived for twenty years finally caught up with me. All that time, I was drinking and doing cocaine Saturday night and then going to church and worshipping Jesus hours later on Sunday. Ever hear of someone hitting rock bottom before they finally have a come-to-Jesus moment? Well, I'd love to say that was me. But the trouble is, I couldn't pick which rock bottom finally did the trick!

When I was preparing to write this book, I knew I had to start with my background. Not just because that's what most people do in biographies and in testimonies, but because you really need to see the mess of a person I was before God changed me and brought me to where I am today. Not just because it makes sense chronologically, which this book will mostly follow, but because I want to glorify God with my words and my story and take you into the depths of where I was when Christ found and rescued me. You need to see where I was at rock bottom, as embarrassing and unflattering to me as that is.

The Lord has done *amazing* things in my life so far in my short time on this earth. Though I'm not as old as many people who write books like this, that doesn't minimize the amount of grace He's shown me or the depths of wickedness He's rescued me from.

But my story is not one meant to glorify sin or show you how rotten I was before committing my life to the Lord. We simply need to start from there so that you can see how He has radically changed me. I used to make fun of Christians. I used to laugh at people like the new me. I used to think the whole Christian life was a big joke. God opened my eyes to this new life, this new world, that's not even here in one sense, the next life.

I wrote an intentionally short book because I wanted to make it a quick and easy read for as many people as possible. I know many people have not gone as far into drugs and alcohol as I have while I also know many have and are currently stuck in their bondage. It's my prayer this book can be placed in their hands as an encouragement and a lifeline. If God can do it for me, He can do it for you as well!

I share some unflattering details about what happened in my family. I absolutely love my mother and my father, and I have a great relationship with both of them. I don't share anything that follows without their permission.

BEGINNINGS

My parents divorced before I was three years old. I have five sisters and no brothers. Alcohol addiction and abuse were normal in my dad's family of origin, so as a result, he demonstrated the same behaviors. He was very abusive toward my mother, and I witnessed many violent outbursts. I could share many of these images that I've never forgotten, but the memories are all too painful.

My father was raised in the Dominican Republic. Child discipline was very strict there, but this was considered the norm for that time and culture. My other siblings and I were disciplined in the same way he had been. My family tree includes heavy drinkers in it, along with my mom. My dad beat her as I watched. I lived with my dad when my parents divorced, and as I grew older, I struggled with anger management and outbursts, which came from his influence. I stayed with him until I was seventeen years old.

Today, my dad today is my best friend, and I love him to pieces. He's not violent anymore, and as I previously stated, I have his permission to share some of these details with you. The following was public knowledge at the time in our community. He was the principal of our high school and found himself in an unfortunate situation that ended poorly for him and for our family. He ended up spending ten years in prison as a result. Around that time, I joined the Air Force and was stationed in the United Kingdom for the next two years. I believe that God himself sheltered me from my dad's trial. This was in 1996, prior to the widespread use of the internet, so most people got their information through the newspaper and local radio and TV news. My mom, who was addicted to both alcohol and crack, gave her life to Christ twenty years ago as of the writing of this book.

I visited my dad once each month in jail, bringing my oldest son with me. To this day, I believe my dad when he claims his innocence and that he did not actually do what he was accused of. He was in the wrong place at the wrong time. He confessed to me some dark secrets that he kept hidden for years, which I believe he was framed for.

When I was in my early twenties while in the air force in the United Kingdom, I wasted a lot of time drinking. After two years, in 1998, I came back home. At twenty years old, I didn't know what I wanted to do with my life. I started working and partying a lot.

This is not the end of my story because I'm obviously still on my journey.

I love God, which is what this book is all about. God has restored my life. Now that I'm saved, I feel as if I've found more joy anyone could ask for. I can't keep the goodness of the Lord concealed within me. It's like a fire in my bones. I have to speak of the Lord and of how good He is. The best way for me to describe it would be like finding gasoline for a dollar—wouldn't you tell everyone?

DRINKING AND DRUGS

I USED to drink at least five days a week, every week. At one point, if I didn't drink for two days, it felt like it had been two weeks. Toward the end of that part of my life, it felt as if an excruciatingly long time had passed between drinks when it really had only been a few days.

I did a lot of stupid things when I drank. I didn't get in trouble every time I drank, but whenever I got in trouble, I had been drinking.

I couldn't even have a social drink because I wasn't a social drinker. It was completely all or nothing. I couldn't have just one beer or one glass of wine; I had to get completely obliterated. Now in hindsight and with a few years of sobriety, I can see this issue for the complete lack of self-discipline that it was. I didn't have a lot of money in those days, so I drank the cheapest beer and the cheapest rum I could get my hands on. I had to have a beer, then a shot; then I had to use cocaine. After that, I needed cigarettes because I needed a smoke while doing cocaine; then I needed marijuana when the cocaine ran out. I needed to have a whole cast and crew of substances if I even started in the direction of inebriation. Every time. I knew exactly what I needed in order to get where I wanted to be.

My cocaine use never progressed to the point of selling any of my personal possessions to buy it nor did I ever steal anything to pay for it. At one point, when I sold my house, I had a large sum of money in the bank, and I would buy an eight-ball every couple of days. If you're unfamiliar with the term, that's equal to 3.5 grams of cocaine or one-eighth of an ounce, also called an eight-ball in street terms. I could do one by myself because it was just *that* normal for me. Cocaine gave me a feeling of a status of superiority, in my mind, that I could have it at my beck and call. In hindsight, I now know it was actually insecurity and inferiority.

If I was mowing the lawn, I called what I was doing yard work, but it was so that I could drink. I'd put on my headphones and do yard work and get hammered. I took time away from my family. I woke up hungover and got to the point where I was vomiting almost every day. Like clockwork, it was just a part of my routine. When I went to brush my teeth, I knew that as soon as I put the toothbrush in my mouth, I had to vomit. So I got in the habit of putting the toothpaste on my brush and then brushing my teeth over the toilet to prepare for what usually happened. It got to the point where I'd have a beer on my way to work at the hospital so that I could try to shake off the hangover. Then at the end of my shift, I couldn't wait to leave work so that I could drink again.

When I went on a dinner date with my ex-wife, we'd each have a glass of wine. I'd drop her off at the house and then, instead of spending time with her, I'd head out because I needed to keep drinking. I always had an excuse, too, such as doing homework or patient charts or whatever I thought up.

I took a lot of time away from my family. I was hungover at my son's games. I'd coach my son's teams half in the bag, thinking that nobody would notice. I hoped they didn't detect the smell because I chewed gum or ate McDonald's on the way over. This was to no avail, however; I heard that alcohol comes out of your pores. I didn't really believe that, but I found out for myself that it's true.

I was very obnoxious in public. If I were to see the old Brian in public now, I'd probably punch him in the face. I used to be really talkative with very loose lips. I loved the night life, especially when I came back from the military. Hardly a night went by where I didn't go out clubbing with a friend. I had a new outfit, went to a new club, same club, old club. It didn't matter; we just went out.

Sometimes I didn't even remember how I got home. I would know by how my car was parked. If it was parked straight, I'd think, "I guess I had a good night." If it was parked crooked, I'd think, "Ugh." I used to drive drunk all the time as if it were no big deal. By this time, I started having blackouts, which became more frequent and lasted longer. Sometimes I went clubbing, and I'd blow my entire paycheck with no recollection of what happened the night before. So I'd call my friends and act like I didn't know what was going on and ask how the night before was. They'd tell me, "Yeah, man, remember what you did?"

I'd respond with, "Oh yeah, yeah," and play along. But I really had no idea what they were talking about. I was fishing for information.

I fell asleep in my car while it was running more than once. Sometimes not even remembering where I was; I woke up in people's houses or women's homes, not even realizing what had happened. I thought all these behaviors were just part of getting drunk. At the time, I didn't realize that I was destroying my life. The greater frequency of those blackouts should have been a warning to me. When they increase, it's past time to stop!

At one or two in the morning after my night of partying was over, I would be wide awake and still trying to chase that high with whatever I could find. I drank cooking wine at times because I had no more alcohol, and the liquor store was closed. I tried to go to bed and just laid there with my ex-wife next to me while I was wide awake. My heart was pounding, fighting my body's attempts to go to sleep. Instead I got up and crept around the house. All of this was very unhealthy.

One night in late 2012, while I was writing a paper with some classmates during my second year of nursing school, I did what I normally did and got drunk. A nearby bar was about to close in fifteen minutes, so we rushed over. When we got there, we bought eight beers each. I drank all mine before closing time, one after the other as if they were water. That was normal behavior.

After that, we headed to a McDonald's restaurant near my home. We hated this particular location because they took too long with our food. But this particular night, we chose to go there because it was close to my house and already late. When I arrived, I was annoyed because nobody was at the drive-through to take my order. I waited about ten minutes idling in my car, hoping someone would take my order, beeping the horn to get someone's attention. But nobody came. I then drove up to the delivery window and knocked, all the while, oblivious to the fact that the store had closed and nobody would be coming to serve me. I pried open the window and yelled, "Hello?" a few times, no one answered. Convinced that nobody was coming, I got out of my car and climbed through the window and started making my own food as if that was acceptable. When I was done, I got back in my car with the freshly made combo meal I made for myself, and began to drive off.

As I was pulling away, I realized I was forgetting a few things. So I put the car in reverse and backed up to the McDonald's window. When I did, I noticed that about ten police officers had just arrived, and they immediately slammed me to the ground and arrested me on the spot. I was charged with trespassing, larceny, and driving while under the influence.

This experience was the beginning of the end. I wound up going to court and lost my license for forty-five days. I had to retake driver's education courses. The local newspaper wrote up what happened, so I was kicked out of the nursing program during my second year because you can't have any open charges against you while in that program. I was dismissed from school until the probation period ended.

The next pivotal moment in my journey before I

completely reached rock bottom came in March 2013. I was coming home from an Easter service with my family, and we discovered a few men in our yard stealing wood. We lived on a street in a cul-de-sac, and this was on the edge of our yard. These people had deliberately come onto our property. We arrived to find a girl behind the wheel of a truck and a man in the driver's seat of another truck. A third man was cutting the wood and throwing it into the back of one of those trucks.

In my anger, I jumped out of my car and confronted them.

"Yo, you're stealing my wood!" I challenged the man with the axe, not thinking about what could happen in this confrontation.

"No, this is city property," he replied. Some back-and-forth conversation ensued between us, but I don't remember it well. I jumped into the back of the truck and started throwing the wood back into my yard, telling my ex-wife to call the cops. While she did, the driver attempted to leave. I didn't want to fall out of the pickup and hurt myself, so I quickly jumped out.

I reached for two chainsaws in the back of the truck. One of the guys saw me and yelled, "Hey, he has your chainsaws!" to the driver. He stopped and parked the truck and came over while the first guy grabbed one of the axes from my hands. The driver took hold of my arm, which had the other one, and struggled to take it from me. I pulled it away from him, and as I did so, he cut his forearm, which started bleeding.

At this moment, the police showed up. The male driver told the cops that I had started swinging the axe at him. The cop believed him, and I was charged with aggravated assault with a deadly weapon.

My problems with alcohol addiction and my corresponding poor decision-making due to the substance abuse, along with violent assault charges, set the stage for everything else that followed. This nearly destroyed my life.

In 2001, I had my first son, Osyris. Shortly after he was born, I started a relationship with a single mother who worked at the daycare center where I took him. She had a two-year old son and six-year old daughter before we'd met. We started out in a healthy relationship, and the first three years were very pleasant. When we began to talk of getting married and moving in together, the relationship changed for the worse. I was abusive to her and repeated the generational pattern of my father. I also continued living a double life, going to church but not really doing anything productive with my life. I was singing hallelujah in church on Sunday morning but was high and drunk by six p.m. "One day, I'll quit," I promised myself, but that day never came.

In 2007, we were supposed to get married. We headed down to Mexico for nine days for a destination wedding, arriving there before all the guests. One night, I got really drunk and made a complete fool of myself, blacking out. I made a horrible mistake. The next morning, my fiancée took her children and left and cancelled the wedding. Family, friends, and people from my job had come down for the ceremony, which was very embarrassing when it all turned out to be for nothing. They were in total shock when I told them it was cancelled. I felt like a total failure. I was so broken and embarrassed. I went out to the beach the night before returning home, and my plan was to cry my eyes out in a pity party for myself. When I sat on the sand, I looked up at the night sky and all of the Lord's stars shining above. Not one tear fell from my eyes. I just prayed and prayed and prayed. I told the Lord, "If you wanted my attention, then you have it. I'm all yours. When I return home I will have nothing left but you." That night, I gave my life to Jesus Christ on that beach in Mexico.

When I got home, I had to move out, get my own apartment, and completely start my life over again. When I went back to work, I was extremely embarrassed because a handful of coworkers had come down for the planned wedding. I knew that everyone in the hospital would eventually find out through gossip as it would spread like wildfire. I took this opportunity to seek the Lord to the best of my ability, but as soon as my situation improved a little, I went right back to my old ways and sinful nature.

People say when you accept Christ that you are saved at that moment, but I don't know how I could consider myself a Christian living the way I was living. There was nothing "Christian" about me. I used to tell people that I was a Christian, and they looked confused since how I presented myself didn't line up with my words or actions. According to some people, I am now fully converted as a disciple and follower of Christ; I was going through the sanctification process. I do believe that the sanctification process is real, but I still wonder if I ever truly accepted Christ if I never had a transformed life. I continued living a double life right into another complete nightmare and downfall. I eventually found myself in the same position: broken, alone, afraid, depressed, drunk, high, defeated, and destroyed.

My girlfriend and I got back together under the condition that I would give up drinking. I promised her I would, but I never truly did and would just go back to alcohol. I would do this many times in the years to come before I truly became sober. I thought I hid my addiction well. I came from a background that demonstrated that manipulation was an accepted character trait. I manipulated everything, which is not hard because again, I came from a family of manipulators.

We ended up getting married two years later, and in 2010, my youngest son, Elias, was born. We bought a home together. A couple of years later, God gave me a vision for catheter underwear while I was working in Interventional Radiology. (I share more on this in depth later as it's an important part of my life story.) I presented the idea to a co-inventor, Hector Arce. We kicked this idea back and forth, and in 2013, we were awarded a patent for it. In October 2013, we were asked to enter an inventors' contest where we won the fan favorite and even received a standing ovation.

That same year, I was in a horrible motor vehicle accident. If I hadn't been wearing my seatbelt, I would have been ejected from the car. I was, however, knocked unconscious. When I awoke, I saw that the car had rolled a few hundred yards and was now upside down, the bottom of the vehicle in flames. I popped off my seatbelt. I could hear the voices of bystanders, but then I blacked out again. When I came to again, people were now pulling me out of the car. I suffered a fractured back and clavicle. I refused to go to the hospital. Since I worked in x-ray, I knew they couldn't do anything to fix a fractured collar bone. So I went home and kept on drinking after the accident. When I woke up the next morning, I still didn't want to go to the hospital. But I was finally persuaded and got a CAT scan. I learned that the T7 of my thoracic spine was fractured. The doctor explained to me that the location of the fracture was due to the pressure placed on it during my near ejection from the car.

Despite my abusive upbringing, a horrible car accident, a DUI charge, a twenty-year alcohol and drug addiction, and a failed attempt at marriage, I can see in hindsight the Lord's hand of protection on me. He still had more for me to do, and as of yet, I was nowhere near able to fulfill my heavenly assignment.

THE DIVORCE

WITHOUT GOING INTO DETAIL, everything changed in my life on January 4, 2014. I can't be specific, and I also want to be careful not to imply anything that can be misinterpreted, but I experienced one of the worst—if not *the* worst—times of my life. False accusations were involved, and rumors were spread about me that led to me getting kicked out of my home. I had criminal charges pressed against me that were eventually dropped after many months, but in the meantime, I lost many friends. Much of 2014 was a very difficult and dark year, including the end of my marriage. Those events started that day.

I had a lot of character flaws that showed up in how I conducted myself. One of the things I realized as I experienced all this is that due to my questionable background—heavy drinking, drugs, sleeping around, and my violent nature, among other things—people didn't believe me when I proclaimed my innocence in this situation either. Where there's smoke, there's fire, and these flaws helped create the reputation that preceded me by this point.

On the one hand, I felt betrayed, but on the other hand, it showed what kind of person I had been up to that point of my life. In some ways, I can't blame anyone, but it was very painful nonetheless. Glory to God, none of us are beyond His redemptive reach. But I'm getting ahead of myself.

I hired a lawyer and paid him a lot of money, and he told me he wouldn't be able to make all the serious charges go away. "Something is going to stick here," were his exact words. I told him that if any of those stuck, I would never be able to work in the medical field again for the rest of my life. He was sympathetic to my plight, but nonetheless he told me that in his thirty-three years of practicing law, he had never been able to get charges like mine dropped. Other people were telling me to take a plea deal, which was also one of his stipulations when he agreed to take me on as a client. All I asked of my lawyer was that he do the best he could. I was going to have to trust in my God "who gave Himself for us, that He might redeem us from every lawless deed and purify for Himself His own special people, zealous for good works" (Titus 2:14).

I didn't want to be around people because of everything that had happened. All my business was very public, and many people were talking about it. I felt deeply ashamed. During this time, I fell into a deep and dark depression. I didn't want to leave my mom's house any more than I had to. I just went to work for eight hours and then came home. I was smoking two packs of cigarettes a day because of the stress I was under. I lost nearly fifty pounds and got really skinny, and I was really unhealthy. My work uniform became too large for me, and I looked like a big boy wearing adult scrubs. I was so depressed and distracted that the thought of buying new scrubs that fit me properly never crossed my mind. I couldn't think or function.

It was a very dark period for me, and everything going on in my head and the shame were more than I could bear. That's why I love the Lord. He removed all the shame from my life as I trusted in Him.

I started hearing from my estranged wife, friends, and other family members that I should just take the plea deal. I continued to resist and reject that idea because I knew I was innocent. Agreeing to a plea meant that I committed the crimes I was being charged with. I decided to take the case to trial and to trust God as my defender. Everybody in my life seemed to be telling me in no uncertain terms that I was being stupid for doing that because of all the chips stacked against me. But by this point, I trusted completely in God.

One night, when I was really feeling the heavy burden of all this on my shoulders, I found myself in the fetal position on the floor at my mom's, begging God to have mercy on me.

"God, you know all things. Nothing is hidden from you. That's what your Word says," I reminded Him. Isn't it interesting how when we're in trouble, we feel compelled to recite God's characteristics and the promises He's made in the written Word back to Him? "Please, please, don't let me go to jail. Don't let me fry for this!" I kept crying. I made a promise to Him—whether rashly and hastily or with pure motives, only He knows—that if He rescued me from all this, I'd quit drinking.

On September 22, 2014, all the charges were dropped. Even the judge expressed his shock. The truth always comes out; the case against me was filled with holes because the truth was coming out. The accusations didn't add up. So I went home to my mom's place, at this point, and I started living the exact same life as before. I signed back up for nursing school the following January 2015 and continued my substance abuse with money in the bank. I was manipulating people all over again. What was worse was that this time, I told people I had quit drinking, but I was still doing my thing on the side. I kept begging my ex-wife to come back. I had incredible faith even though I was still drinking and doing drugs at that time.

I returned to school, but I was profoundly arrogant as well. I had money from the accident I was in in 2013 and from selling the house I had shared with my ex-wife. Aside from going to nursing school, however, I began the year 2015 partying it up and bought a new car while working at paying off all our bills and continuing my attempts to win back my ex-wife.

Even though the charges filed against me were dropped that September, my life only became worse as I spiraled further out of control into drinking, drugs, and partying.

At this point, my mother came home from work and found me in the fetal position, crying after the divorce was finalized. I realized my ex-wife had moved on with another man for good. My mom just started laying it on me while I was there on the floor. I was in the same exact spot where I had wept when I made my vow to God about getting sober if He dropped the charges.

"You're still crying because you never changed. You never fulfilled the promise you made to God. You promised Him if He dropped all those charges, you'd quit drinking, and you never did." She told me other things as well, but that was the main point.

At that moment, a lightbulb went off, and I told her, "Oh, wow. I didn't realize God was listening." My lawyer had even admitted that it was a miracle when my charges were dropped. He had never seen those types of charges dismissed in his entire thirty-three-year career. He told me he was shocked to see me walk out of the courthouse as a free man. Yet here I was, not honoring the promise I made to the Lord and back to the old lifestyle I was living when I had made that vow, digging my hole deeper.

The Lord reminded me of this through my dear mom.

I think one of the most beautiful things in this life is watching God turn something negative into something positive. I was certain that I was not going to get divorced. My faith for my marriage was so strong. I believe today that my faith in God is very high because God saw how much faith I had in Him even when it didn't look like my situation would work out. I still believed even though I ended up getting divorced. God still knows my heart and knows how much I believed in his life-changing ability. I would have cut my arm off in a bet saying, "There's no way God's going to allow this divorce to happen." Even though it didn't work out like I believed it would, God turned the negative into a positive. He saw and showed me how much I had fully put my trust and faith in Him and showed me how much my relationship with Him had deepened after He reconciled my life with His.

I also had unshakable faith that I would get back together with my ex-wife. One of the first Scripture passages I ever learned and memorized was Joel 2:25, which is a verse about God's restoration. I believed the promise that said that God would restore what the locusts had eaten, and I applied it to my own life. Though I had not fully and unconditionally surrendered my life to Jesus yet, I had started memorizing Scriptures like this one.

The devil would use that against me and torment me. "Come on, God restores, right? He's going to restore your family, isn't he?" The devil would remind me of the natural circumstances and how they didn't look like what I felt God had promised me.

I kept begging my ex-wife to come back to me. I had incredible faith, even though I was still drinking and doing drugs. I was believing God for complete restoration in our marriage, but I still handled things horribly. I basically stalked her; I called her excessively on the phone. I found out where she was or where she was going to be so that I could randomly show up. It was very unhealthy. I heard the devil telling me, "She's going to come back. You just gotta pursue her. Remember God's promise!" God did promise that He would restore, but He restored *me*. I learned that He will restore what He wants to restore, when and how He wants to, not what I want Him to restore. And so in retrospect, God did restore. He restored my relationship with Him. He essentially restored me.

At this point, I was two years into a four-year nursing program. Although I had to drop out because of the case filed against me, I was still confident I'd get back into the program in 2015, which I eventually did.

I also had high hopes that maybe the divorce would not happen because my ex-wife had let the divorce papers expire. But then she re-filed the papers. We finally got divorced in August of 2015.

My life was in a state of depression for three years from 2014–2016. During that time, I got on social media like everybody else and tried to fix my image. I started on Instagram and was sucked into posting about becoming a nurse and posted materialistic updates about clothes I bought and my new car. My Instagram feed reflected a shallow existence and unimportant activity in my life. Like many who post in this way, I was very insecure because I didn't know who I was. I didn't yet understand the blood of Christ that takes away shame and gives life. I didn't yet know about eternal life like I do now. I thought this was the end of my life and that this was how I was going to go out.

The symptoms of depression are very real. They're heavy, demonic and opposite from God. Jesus came to give life abundantly, and God is the Father of light. He reversed all my shame and depression, and now that stuff is fuel for me to serve God. The Word of Christ liberated me in both the physical and spiritual sense. All the pain and everything I went through helps give me the strength to preach. God used it all and made beauty from my ashes and strength from my weakness. He gave me a brand new life, just like He said He would in a vision that I later had in the living room.

I need to back up and clarify something about my divorce. Even though I had signed the papers and agreed to a divorce, I still loved my ex-wife and wasn't done with our marriage. I still had faith and hope that the situation would change. I saw her after the proceedings and got on my hands and knees and begged for another chance. She told me the alcohol was a deal breaker. She had no confidence whatsoever that I would quit drinking. I told her I would, and for a while, I truly did. But one day, she came by my house to drop off our son, and I couldn't let her see my face because I was hungover. She asked me one last time if I was drinking, and I confessed that I was. That was it.

I went through a lot of dark thoughts, emotions, and other horrible experiences, but I want to respect her and to not give the devil any credit that he doesn't deserve. But I will say that I was suicidal and even homicidal. I started having visions of committing horrible crimes and hurting myself and others. That's when I knew I was in danger. In those days, I also could have filled up a few tanks with the tears of hurt and sorrow I shed. I could not stop crying. At work, I could hold it together when I was with patients, but as soon as I was out of their view for even a few seconds, I'd let the tears flow. Then I'd wipe off my face and turn around to help them get situated. As soon as I had another free moment, the tears would flow again. I was a broken man and easily lost fifty pounds in those first few months.

On the same day my divorce was finalized, as I left the courtroom, my first son, Osyris, called me on my cell phone. He told me his mom had kicked him out and that he was at his grandma's (my mother's) where I was staying at the time. This was obviously a bright encouraging spot because of the difficulties in the relationship between me and his mother. I had fought to see him over the years, and now I was finally going to live with him. I hadn't specifically asked or prayed about this, but God orchestrated this turn of events. I believe the Lord gave me my son because He knew I was about to go through fire. I thank God for my son because I didn't want him to see me drinking. I wanted to break that generational curse. I wanted to stop the alcoholism in my family. I knew if I broke my promise one more time, I would be showing my son that it's okay to break the promises you make to God.

In the months after the divorce, life was incredibly difficult, and so many times, I wanted to drink. That voice would whisper in my ear, "It's okay; he's in bed. Go get a drink, he won't know. You'll be sober by the time he sees you." I would say no to these impulses. I wanted to show him that when you make a commitment to God, you keep it!

One night, during one of those intense moments when I wanted to relieve the agony I was experiencing and have a drink, Jesus showed up. He came close to me and drew a circle around my face with his hand. When he did this, I told Him, "Lord, I don't want to take my life." I said this because I kept seeing in my mind's eye my son waking up and finding me in a pool of blood. I didn't want to do that to him. My father told me that he hadn't killed himself when he was convicted and went to prison because he knew the impact it would have on me, his son. He told me that if he had killed himself, then I would kill myself one day too. I vowed that I would not kill myself because I knew the cycle would continue, and I did not want my son to kill himself one day either.

I told myself, "Brian, you're being selfish. You got yourself into this mess, and now you're going to take your life and leave your son alone? You're such a selfish b*****d!" I just kept visualizing his face and imagining him finding me dead in a pool of my own blood. It was unbearable.

The Lord told me to go into my bedroom and shut the door where I laid on the floor. I heard God say to me, "Tell me everything that you've done. Go through your entire life." That's what I did. I went through every moment I remembered from my teen years until that day in my bedroom as best as I could. Whenever I tried blaming somebody else, God told me, "No, no, no. Don't talk to me about anybody else. Just talk to me about you." I then recalled what I said and did, what I tried to hide or manipulate. Whenever I forgot and began blaming someone else or when I began giving excuses for my actions, God gently nudged me to take responsibility for my own actions during this divine reckoning with Him.

I love that God did this that night. In His questioning, He made me focus on just my own behavior and actions. I could see clearly like never before just how much alcohol had played a key role in each of these pivotal moments in my life, beginning when I started drinking at seventeen.

After this time ended, I came out of my room and sat on the living room couch. I had this profound revelation where I thought, "I'm actually going to quit drinking now."

That's when Jesus came to me. I cried and told the Lord, "Please stop what you're doing! I can't take it anymore."

The Lord told me, "If you don't stop drinking, I'm going to do more."

At that, I pleaded with Him to stop. He responded by telling me, "This is it, Brian. I have more."

I said, "Lord, I've tried to quit drinking so many times, and I couldn't do it." That's when He drew that circle around my face. The tip of His finger was closer to my eyes than the rest of His hand, almost in 3-D fashion. He just kept circling from left to right, and He said to me, "I can't work with you in this condition. You won't fit into what I'm trying to do as long as your mind is cloudy. I can't work with people like that."

"Lord, I can't do it! I've tried to quit so many times before," I responded, weeping.

"Yes, you can," The Lord answered.

"How do you know?" I asked.

"Because now I'm going to give you my Spirit!"

At that moment, He went across the street and turned around. He was standing next to a tree. It was almost as if He waited for me to come to Him. He said to me, "If you cross this street, I'll take care of the rest. But I'm not going to remove the drugs and the alcohol from you. You'll have to do that on your own."

He kept waving at me to come, and I knew in my spirit that crossing the street meant that I was crossing into sobriety. The next day, I got high and drunk one more time, and I felt lower than low. I wept and prayed and cried out to God and said, "I don't want this anymore!" That was it.

As I think back over this while writing, I'm just so angry at the devil: so angry that he deceived me and caused me to hurt my family and get a divorce. He tricked me into thinking the only way I was going to live the rest of my life was as a drunk. I thought that was it, but Jesus Christ gave me hope. I know now there's another life. I saw it. God showed me the kingdom of heaven. I went outside for six months straight, and I could see it in the sky. I can see it best at night. I know its color, location, and size, and I cross-referenced it all with Scripture. The only reason I believe what I'm seeing is because the Bible talks about it. That's why I'm now going so hard for and after Jesus.

When I had seven days of sobriety, I went to a first-time testimonial night at my church. Interestingly, I went with my one of my best friends, Medwin Melendez, who was also my drinking buddy but almost didn't come. I grabbed the mic and told everybody there that I was done, tired, and sick and tired of being sick and tired. Then I literally dropped the mic, got on my knees, and said, "From this day forward, I'm delivered. I'm free!" I never drank again after that night.

I've been sober ever since September 26, 2015. At the time of this writing, it's been three-and-a-half years of complete sobriety as well as freedom from all the drugs I used to do, including smoking cigarettes. Glory to God! The Lord took care of everything. He did everything that He said He would do. I still suffer some of the consequences and am working out issues from my old life. I am a saint because the Lord says I am one, but I rejoice in the Lord, knowing that at the very least, I killed the head of that snake with His help. I can now focus on the smaller tasks of the sanctification process.

THE NURSING EXAM

I GRADUATED with honors in December 2015. I was so proud of this accomplishment because I had taken two years off to deal with all the criminal charges and had gone through a difficult divorce. I repeatedly heard that nobody who quits ever finishes nursing school because it's extremely challenging. This was significant because I felt like if I could graduate from this program after everything I had been through up to that time, then I could do anything I set my mind to. I believe only someone who has died to themselves in this realm can do this because nursing school takes such a heavy toll on your life. Even without the struggles, it's difficult! That's why I serve God the way I do: with so much passion and intensity. If He can get me through that, then He can straight up get me through anything.

My reputation was incredibly damaged after the previous year, and the whole ordeal really humbled me. I was so arrogant in my former life. I was so insecure, but I didn't realize it. I understand now that arrogance is a cover-up for deep-rooted issues I had from growing up, and the recent events of my life really pushed the arrogance to the surface of everything I did. Second Corinthians 12:7 mentions that Paul had a messenger of Satan tormenting him. Micah 7:19 also says that God forgets our sins and iniquities, but I believe the consequences will remain. I was reminded of them daily. Isaiah 66:9 says, "I will not allow pain without producing purpose," and He will turn everything the devil tried to do to me for His glory (author's paraphrase).

Many rumors were being spread about me within the circle of friends I thought I had. The hardest part was that I had nobody to believe me. Even my parents doubted me and repeatedly asked me about the stories. I see now that this was a great opportunity from God to just seek His approval. It still took a toll on me, but it was my fault. I had some major character issues that I had been in denial about for years. They had all come to a head during this time in my life. To be honest, I still have minor struggles here and there, but the Lord gives me the victory over these. The Lord Jesus turned the entire downfall into a master plan. I've become better at embracing my past. I love the person the Lord has turned me into, and I realize I couldn't have moved into my purpose if I hadn't gone through what I've been through.

It was hard because, at the time, I didn't want to show my face anywhere in public. I didn't leave my mom's apartment for three or four months. But God is a God of justice, and in my actual innocence, whether anybody believed me or not, Jesus made things right. I'm very thankful for Xavier Veras. I didn't even know this guy, but he kept befriending me. I opened up my feelings to him one day and he just kept telling me, "Everything is going to work out in your favor." It didn't matter what I was telling him was going on; his response was always the same. He invited me out of the house one day to run an errand. He forced me to go with him and said he would pull me out of my mother's apartment if I didn't go. I went, and my life started to get better from that day on.

In February 2016, I failed the nursing school license exam—the first time I had ever failed any exam in my life. I had no money left and didn't know what I would do to survive. I had budgeted all that money from the house, thinking that I would pass the nursing exam on the spot. I had money from a car accident and the sale of the home we used to live in. My mind was in such disarray, I couldn't focus, and all my focus was on getting my ex-wife back. It was the hardest exam I'd ever taken, and I failed it. I was so scared because I had sole custody of my oldest son Osyris, who was fourteen at the time and living with me. I had to go on welfare just to keep food on the table. This was truly humbling because the old Brian used to talk so much trash about people who went on welfare, and now here I was, needing it myself. I love that about God; He just continues to humble me. I was in tears in the welfare office, looking around at all the people and seeing myself now as one of them. I gave the glory to God for who He says He is: a provider. I had a fridge full of food for me and my two boys. Thank you, Lord.

I had to wait forty-five days before I could retake the licensing exam, so I took it again in April but failed it a second time. I still had no money, and I didn't know anybody I could borrow from. At this point, broken and humbled further as I was, I cried out to God and confessed to Him that if He wanted to back me into a corner so that I had nothing to depend on except Him, then I would submit to that.

I felt that God must be doing something in my life, and I had increasing faith that He would take care of me and my son. At that time, God showed me heaven: the location, size, and colors of the kingdom of heaven. I asked Jesus if I could show it to my sons. After the Lord confirmed to me that what I was seeing was from Him, He gave me permission to do so. We went out every night and looked at it and talked about various aspects of heaven in the sky. We can still see it to this day, and we can see it the clearest at night. I kept researching Scripture at that time, and I was basically lovesick with seeking God.

I believe the reason I failed my nursing exam is because the only thing I could do was spend time with Him and keep digging into His word (and also my nursing books) for months. I didn't watch any TV or waste time on any sort of entertainment. He backed me into a corner where I had to focus on Him and His will for my life. I'm so thankful that I failed those two licensing exams even though, at the time, I was unsure of the exact course of my life. I needed to trust God even when I couldn't see what He was doing at the time. Who would've thought I'd be writing a book about this experience when I chose to lock myself in my apartment and seek His presence?

When it comes to my passion for studying this, I know there is no death in Christ, but where you'll spend eternity matters. We're spiritual beings who are having a human experience not humans who are having a spiritual experience. We'll live forever in one of two locations: the "VIP Room" or the "Boom Boom Room." Of course, I'm referring to Heaven and Hell. We've been lied to about our identity and our reason for being here on earth. The devil is such a liar, and he lies to all of us, which is why so many of us don't know who we are. I know who I am because God told me who I am in His Word.

I just want to wage warfare through Jesus Christ against the devil's lies for the rest of my life, which is why I spread the gospel with so much passion and determination. It's such a revelation of truth. I used to be so materialistic and shallow. I thought life was about owning a great 401K plan and a huge house with bright green grass, sprinklers, and a four-car garage with fancy cars, but I was insecure and wanted to use material possessions to cover up my insecurities and darkness. I no longer care about these things, and the less I care about material items, the more He blesses me with them. It's like the parable of the talents; I just grow whatever He gives me and then give it right back to Him, His people, and His churches. It's all for Jesus. I just want to make an impact for Jesus while I'm here. When my train arrives, I want to depart. But I digress.

After He showed me the kingdom of heaven, I saw this video of Todd White singing in an airport to random people going by while he waited for his flight. The Holy Spirit used him to show me this: *That's* how we're supposed to be! We're supposed to be outwardly expressive, and by nature, I'm a lot like that evangelist. It took a lot of practice to be able to speak about what Jesus was doing in my life without coming across as bragging. I didn't know how to properly express myself or word things when I wanted to glorify God. I tried to glorify God with what I said, but I couldn't share what I meant, so I looked as if I was glorifying myself. People thought I was making it all about me, which was never my intention. I've learned to shy away from using the word "I" or "me" when speaking about the Lord in order to keep the focus on Him at all times. I might bring attention to myself but only to give glory to God. Perhaps this was true, and in my new-found zeal, I could have been unintentionally coming across as self-promoting. What God has done in me is like a fire on my tongue, and I can't stop talking about Jesus and the goodness He desires to provide to those who surrender to His will in their lives. I needed an outlet to express myself because I couldn't contain it any longer. One of my patients was the last person to confirm the Lord wanted me to start posting inspirational videos on Facebook, and I decided to try it. That ended up paying great dividends for the reign and rule of God, but I'm getting ahead of my story.

On July 5, 2016, I passed the nursing exam—the third time's the charm, they say—and opened CathWear one month later. This is significant because, in 2013, when I still was living the double life of church-goer and addict in the world, I invented and patented this invention, and I told God that if He grows it, I would give it back to Him. I didn't realize until later in my life that the fires I went through were actually God helping me to fulfill this commitment I made to Him. Now, in 2016, on the other side of deliverance and salvation, since I've started the business, I remembered my commitment to the Lord three years earlier.

Shortly afterward, I laid hands on a condemned building near where I was attending Bible school and prayed that my inventions will generate revenue to donate the money to fix the school so that they could use it to advance the reign and rule of God. I prayed that when He multiplied CathWear, I'd give $1.2 million to the school to buy it, which is one reason I believe CathWear is the success it is today. In an upcoming chapter, I will elaborate more on the amazing journey this invention has been so far.

It's worth noting another detail right here. In 2015, just one month before the charges against me were dropped, I invented a surgical clip and sold it to Cook Medical, which is based in Indiana. They are still working on finalizing the design to then sell across the earth. Out of that one invention, I own three American patents and one European patent. It's been amazing to see the doors that God has opened for me. CathWear has had so much publicity without even spending a penny on advertising. We've been featured in the local newspaper; we were on the cover of a magazine, featured in another one, interviewed on the radio on two occasions, and won first place at an invention contest. The best part is that it's all for Jesus to bring Him glory for restoring my broken life.

CATHWEAR

I EARNED my degree in Radiology, and for a while, I worked in Interventional Radiology. I wanted to invent a device to help my youngest son, Elias, who was just an infant. He was ill and was having difficulty breathing because of mucous build up. He sounded as if he were suffocating, and I was worried he might die in his sleep. He made this very loud snorting noise when he tried to inhale. One day, I went into the operating room where I worked, found some equipment, and made a suction-like device to suck mucous from his mouth with a long straw. I was in inventor mode and wanted to create and patent the design, but when I showed it to his pediatrician at the time, she shot down the idea. She warned me I'd need FDA approval. She thought it was too close to the child's nose, and she discouraged me in several other ways. That same device is now sold in Walmart and similar stores worldwide because someone else invented and patented it. I learned my lesson, and I was not going to let an idea or an inspired invention get away from me ever again.

During that season, while I was still in the inventor mindset, I saw a patient with a catheter and leg bag strapped around his leg with Velcro or elastic straps. These straps were not secure, so the bag slid up and down the leg. Patients tended to over-tighten them to avoid any embarrassing moments of the bag being exposed through their clothes. The plastic from the leg bag touches the skin, creating sweating and skin irritation. The bags also increase the risk of circulatory issues. On top of that, the straps themselves also become unsanitary, creating infections from rashes. This means that they can't wear shorts, skirts, or dresses in the warm weather. They can't go golfing, spend time outside with their family, or do other activities. The leg bags significantly reduce the quality of life for the patients. So patients then become frustrated because sometimes excessive tubing is inadvertently pulled out, and when it does, they must come back and have it replaced, resulting in a delay to their recovery and treatment and increased expenses.

One day, I saw a patient come in and drop his pants. All the tubing was everywhere. The Lord Jesus gave me a vision for undergarments like shorts with pockets for the drainage bags and holes so that the tubing could be kept out of the way. I know Jesus gave me the vision because this invention is so advanced that it is impossible for me to have thought of it on my own. I encounter doctors with PhDs from Harvard who have asked themselves why they didn't think of this device or why didn't someone else think of it since it is so practical.

I ended up presenting the vision to my friend Hector Arce, and we split the cost of the patent. On July 16th, 2013, we were awarded the patent. Shortly after that, we entered a patent-and-invention contest and won. One of the judges in the contest had a leg bag twenty years previously and said he couldn't believe that no one had invented such a device since then. At the time, we were in nursing school, and the dean of nursing also expressed her surprise that nobody had done it yet, but she was not surprised that a nurse came up with the idea. Nurses see these things from a patient's perspective, giving them an idea of the type of care that patients need. At the time, we hadn't yet come up with the name CathWear, and if I remember correctly, we were calling it Drainage Partner. In late 2013, we were instructed to change the name, and I'm sure you'd agree that Cath-

Wear is a much better name! After that, much of what I previously shared happened. For all intents and purposes, CathWear sat on the shelf for over two years as I came out of that cave and passed my nursing license exam.

One month after I opened CathWear, I reached out to my high school friend Edwin Alvarez, who I had not seen since 2006. The last time I saw him, I gave him what turned out to be a prophetic word. "Edwin, I don't know what it is about you, but I feel like one day, we're going to be working together, and whatever it is, it's going to be big." The project ended up being this.

After we won the invention contest, we were trying to sell the idea, but we couldn't generate enough of a buzz around the design. I now see the Lord's will for the project because CathWear and many other companies are being used to inspire the city of Lawrence, Massachusetts, during these times of revival. The design is also allowing the Lord's name to further enter corporate sectors. The counsel we received was to grow the business and then sell it once we created a market for it. I personally didn't want to be involved in the business aspect of running a company, as odd as that sounds. I wanted to work directly with patients, their families, and doctors and focus on selling the invention through speaking engagements and pitches. I learned early in my walk with the Lord to identify my areas of weakness and find help in those areas. Around that time, I ran into Edwin, who is also a Christian, and told him all about where I was with the design and showed him the patent. He has his master's degree in business, so he naturally did his research on it. In fact, he initially tried to debunk it; he believed that it was a brilliant and practical idea, not to mention an obvious one. Once he learned about it, he said there was no way that the product didn't already exist. Edwin spent two days trying to find a similar patent and couldn't find anything even remotely close. He decided to come on board when he found nothing and took the shell of a business plan I had. He just ran with it and helped me turn it into an international company.

We were also working on some logo ideas, and Edwin suggested having a contest at Northern Essex Community College where I had earned my radiology degree. We ran the contest very similarly to the invention contest we had won; we presented it to their computer design department and judged all the designs from the students. I kept getting a vision of a cross on the logo. I was going to find a way to put a cross on the logo no matter what. Per the contract, I had the final say regarding the company image. All I wanted to do was bring glory to God with every part of my life. I had committed the logo to the Lord although I didn't know exactly what it would look like. But the cross was important, even if it was a watermark. I wanted to honor God with this business since He had given me the vision for the original invention. In 2013, when we were awarded the patent, I presented it to God. As I already mentioned, that was when I told the Lord Jesus that if He made this project grow, then I would buy Pastor Rick a new church with it. For all I know, the entire nightmare I went through was designed to put me in the right frame of mind so that I could focus on this promise I made to the Lord, and in turn, New Life Christian Church and Pastor Rick Amendola.

We received many logo submissions from the contest, but Edwin and I didn't really like them. Edwin pointed out one with a cross that he liked. I was confused because I didn't see any such logo. Edwin didn't know yet about my vision from the Lord of the logo with a cross, so I looked again at the PDF file with the fifteen logos we had received. I saw the logo there that we are now using today. I freaked out.

"That's it!" I said. And to top it off, the woman who designed it had the last name of Miracle. We decided to use her design for our logo and run with it. At that point, we started travelling more and doing presentations about the product and growing the business.

It has been an awesome journey so far, but that doesn't mean it has been easy. This company has faced a lot of obstacles and resistance due to my relentlessness in spreading the gospel, sharing about God on social media, and talking about Jesus every chance I get. God has this company that He's given me and put me in charge of. I see myself as just managing what's in front of me. I have always said that if I side with the Lord Jesus, I will always land on my feet.

One day, I was in the shower where the Holy Spirit often speaks to me. At the time, I had been reading Ephesians in preparation for my first time preaching on a Sunday morning. I was going to speak on chapter six about the armor of God, in particular, the shield of faith. This subject had been on my heart for a month.

The Holy Spirit said to me, "Hey, Brian, remember the cross on the logo? I gave it to you."

I said, "Okay."

"Well, what about the shield?" He asked me.

"What about it?"

"Brian, the shield in Ephesians that you're studying right now." This lit something in me, you see, because the shield on the logo was always a pocket to hold the leg bags in my mind because that's how the actual underwear look.

"That's *my* logo," the Lord explained further. "That's the cross at Calvary and the shield of faith. So declare that this is a Christian-based company." That was an easy command to obey as I've always wanted to have a Christian-based company.

We had a bunch of deals with the military we were still waiting on and thought they had gone stale. I had not received a single response. At this point, I went on Facebook and posted on the CathWear business page that it was a Christian-based company. I explained the logo's purpose and stated that we believe in the Father, the Son, and the Holy Spirit and that Jesus Christ died on that cross for our sins and that He's the only way to heaven. I further explained that the shield represents faith and that we have to put our faith in him to deliver the best quality product possible. I concluded the post by saying that whatever comes our way, we'll continue to conduct ourselves with integrity and provide the best possible product and trust God with the results.

I posted that update without discussing it with any of my business partners, but that was my part of the contract. I had negotiated the business contract to make sure I would always have control of the image of the company because I wanted to make sure that we could always glorify God in everything we did. As a result, Edwin and I argued for two days about the post. He told me that I couldn't post that and that I was taking this too far among similar concerns. He pointed out to me the heat that many companies come under for wearing their faith on their sleeves. After two days, we made peace with each other over it. I apologized for not running it by him before posting on social media. He responded with the following, which I paraphrase.

"No, you know what Brian? To be honest with you, I'm truly just amazed in a sense. I just don't have the guts to do what you're doing for God, and I admire that about you. I just couldn't do it, and part of my reaction is because I've never seen anybody as on fire for God as you are."

The next day, after reconciling with my business partner, we were flooded with the email responses from the military we had been waiting on. Each and every facility we wanted to speak to but couldn't get a hold of responded to us. We started setting up meetings and cracked that door into the military with CathWear wide open.

Let me say it again: When you side with God, everything turns out right!

BIBLE COLLEGE

I ENROLLED in Bible school in September of 2015, only one month into sobriety, four months before nursing school ended. At the time, I had no idea why I did so. I just went online and registered. I did an accelerated course in nursing school that I finished in December 2015 and not the following May the way most people would. After I graduated, I had no classes for a week, and I wasn't working either. I only had a few dollars in the bank, and I was bored out of my mind. As much as I complained about nursing school, I kind of missed it. The Holy Spirit told me, "Why don't you give me a chance? Why don't you just go to Bible college?"

I was a bit puzzled and responded, "Why would I go to the Bible college?"

"Why don't you just go and see what happens?" He

responded. "Just sign up for a class. What can it hurt? You know you're good at school. You already have two degrees. You know how to study. Just sign up for one class, Brian, and see what happens."

I decided to drive to the school since I was doing nothing at home. I signed up for one class and immediately started that following January. I had now been sober for five months, and I was emotionally broken. North Point Bible College has church services every school day on campus at 11:00 a.m., so I went from Monday–Thursday without fail. I had decided to immerse myself in the presence of Jesus, and I had a desire to know what He was really like. I wanted to know if it was all hype. I wanted to see what my life would be like if I surrendered it all to Him. I wanted to know what it meant to be a servant of Christ. I wanted to turn everything that had happened to me into a positive blessing. I wanted a brand-new life as His Word says. So I simply immersed myself in the presence of God. I just wanted to be around Him. I couldn't stop reading my Bible, and I couldn't stop praising Him. I'm so passionate about my praise because I just wanted to know His goodness and see Him heal me. I kept crying out and praising Him; I kept trusting in Him. Even though I was financially broke, I was still giving $40.00 per week to offerings, which, at that time, was a large amount of money to me. I knew what working for the devil felt like and what darkness was. This question constantly rattled in my head, "What does it feel like to serve and live for Jesus?"

Today, I'm still taking classes, albeit at a different Bible school, and still studying to be a pastor. I will be finished in approximately one year after this book is released. God has never allowed me to grow cold in my pursuit of Him. Every time something negative has happened, every time something has come up, it has pushed me toward Christ. The devil overplays his hand when he messes with me because every time he hurts me, I scream "Hallelujah!" even louder. Every time a door is closed or somebody tries to bother me, I just praise and worship God even more. I spread the gospel more; I post more inspirational pictures and comments on Facebook.

I believe in praising and worshipping God in private and in public and bathing in His presence. I've seen His goodness and grace upon my life. I don't give any credit to the devil. I never say things like, "The devil is testing me today." He has no say over my life. He's a liar and an accuser. I never speak of him unless I'm calling him out on his deception. I only speak to him with Scripture. That's the only thing the devil is afraid of: Jesus and His Word. He's a rat, and he'll take any publicity he can get even if it's negative. I give all glory to God for anything that happens in my life. I don't see anything as bad or negative anymore. All I see is the goodness of the Lord in my life. I praise Him because He is holy and worthy. I choose to magnify the name of the Lord.

I still struggle, and God's Spirit convicts me and asks, "Why are you doing that?" I'm not perfect, and He's not seeking perfection, but man, I'm trying my best to stay hot with His grace! People sometimes make comments, such as, "You're just hot now because you just started." But at the time of this writing, I'm going on four years of running this race without slowing down!

HEROIN EPIDEMIC

IN 2018, the heroin epidemic hit an all-time high here in the Merrimack Valley where I live. This region consists of five or six towns, and Lawrence is the largest city among them. In March 2018, I made a series of videos on Facebook with my friend Eric Diaz about this. I shared how Christians need to rise to the occasion to spread the gospel, and I used the words "heroin epidemic." Seven days later, after posting the last video, President Donald Trump came and spoke in this region on television. To my shock, he rightfully declared this a heroin epidemic. We were called the center of the heroin epidemic, cesspool, and pit stop for New Hampshire. The President of the United States agreed with what I had been saying in these videos, confirming these words were from God and not my own message.

When I heard the President's speech, I felt very frustrated that my hometown was getting kicked in the teeth like that, but I also heard the Holy Spirit say to me that "the stage has been set." Our free will and sin allows circumstances to become really bad. God turns all things into good for those who love Him. He uses these situations so that His power can be shown through the circumstance. (See the story of Pharaoh in Exodus 1–14.)

The next day, I was in the kitchen, randomly sweeping the floor, wearing just my underwear and a T-shirt, and the videos the Holy Spirit inspired us to make along with the president's message popped into my head. I started crying and was overcome with anxiety but also felt very peaceful at the same time. It's difficult to explain; the Holy Ghost was downloading information right into my spirit. The message was for a video directed specifically at drug dealers, proclaiming that the Lord was going to set the captives free. My initial reaction was, *"No way!"*

I swept the same spot over and over as the video and Scriptures were being illuminated in my mind. I started crying and speaking in tongues, begging the Lord to let this not be from Him and to just let it be my imagination. I kept praying about it, telling God "No, no, no!

Please let this be my own silly idea. If it was my idea, it won't come to pass. Why would you have me do that?" I repeatedly asked Him that day and the days following. With everything I had previously gone through during my fiery trial, I wanted to be sure my motives were pure. I didn't want people to see the video and think, "Who is this dude, and who does he think he is? Isn't this the guy who was accused of all those things a few years ago?" When I came to the realization that I'd better obey God, I started to think about how I was going to structure the videos. My only desire was to do the will of the Father.

I almost didn't do the video because I was afraid. I said, "No, God, I'll do it next week." And the Lord suggested to me, "Why don't you do it on Resurrection Weekend when I'm at the forefront of everybody's mind? I want it done now." I kept trying to find reasons to put it off.

I was crying the entire week. I had anxiety. I felt sick. I wondered what I would do and thought it was just my imagination. I had ideas float into my head that perhaps I didn't really hear from God about doing the video, and in my heart, I was resistant. I was in my prayer room where I spent most of my time since I reconciled my relationship with the Lord, and I was praying in silence for hours. I couldn't control my tears (and fears), but I felt this sense of peace, so I knew this was the Lord's will. I'm reminded of the Scripture in Hebrews 13:6, "So we may boldly say: 'The LORD is my helper; I will not fear. What can man do to me?'"

Two weeks before all of this happened, Chris Benitez, a brother in Christ, called me on Messenger out of the blue and asked if he could pray for me. He told me he was reading a book called *It's Happening Now* by Michael McDowell, which stated that any time someone mentions the word "revival," that person needs support because they're receiving information directly from the throne of God

The prophetic video was posted to my Facebook page on Saturday, March 31, 2018. The Thursday before that, the Holy Spirit spoke to me and said "If you do this, I'll give you something. If you do this for me, I'll do something for you. If you decide against it, I will still love you. You have been asking me over and over to use you to do my will, and here's your chance. You have been begging me for a double portion for over two years, and I'm ready to use you." That was it, and I stopped crying right on the spot, and it was done. I called the other brothers up who I'd be doing this video with. I told them I was ready, and now it was time to move. I didn't even so much as bat an eye over doing the video any longer. I had peace, and I started sharpening up the outline I had been preparing to use, making sure everything in it was okay. I rehearsed it as well.

Chris introduced me to Weylin Vidal, another brother with a company named Kingdom Prints. Around this time, Weylin was advertising a painting with the picture of a lion on it. My friend Eric Diaz had asked me what I thought of this painting over two months prior. In all honesty, I didn't particularly care for the drawing itself nor did I see what was written on it. One day, Eric and I went to the Kingdom Prints office, praying for God to open doors and to expand his territory and business operations. As a result, my relationship with both Chris and Weylin started developing.

For this prophetic video, God put Proverbs 13:11 on my heart which says, "Wealth gained by dishonesty will be diminished, but he who gathers by labor will increase."

God started downloading more information into my spirit. Proverbs 28:1 says, "The wicked flee when no one pursues, but the righteous are bold as a lion." The Lord finally gave me Psalm 20:7–9. "Some trust in chariots and some in horses; but we will remember the name of the Lord our God. They have bowed down and fallen; but we have risen and stand upright. Save, Lord! May the King answer us when we call."

In the video, I planned on standing on the stage at

the Common Park in Lawrence, Massachusetts, on Friday of that week and pray over it before I went there Saturday morning. That Friday, I was fasting — no water or food all day — because I wanted to be covered by the blood of Christ. I wanted to be in top spiritual shape. I knew I would be making a declaration to a bunch of heroin dealers, and I thought that I might lose my life after this. I still felt no fear and was at peace. I honestly didn't know what to think or expect if I was going to wage spiritual warfare on a level like this. If you think about it, it was so bizarre to make a video like that and think that it was from God. I mean, who does that? Who tells the drug dealers to cease and desist? Mentioning the Lord to a drug dealer who is a non-believer is like mentioning the boogeyman.

I previously mentioned to Chris that I was going to go on the stage and pray at ten o'clock on Friday night that week, but I totally forgot about it until Chris called me up. I received the phone call from him at 9:30 p.m., asking me if I was still going to go. I had just come home from church and was getting undressed when I answered. I had no idea why he was calling. He lives ninety minutes away from me. I was embarrassed when I realized I had forgotten all about our prayer time and that this was why he called. Chris was patient with me and asked me to let him know if I was still going to go, and I replied in the affirmative. I hurried, changed, and drove down there so that I could make it by 10:00 p.m. I may or may have not been respecting the speed limit, only God knows! I talked with Chris on the phone on my way there, and he told me, "I'm here."

"You're 'here' where?" I asked, a bit puzzled.

"I'm here, at the stage," he responded.

"Wow, you drove an hour and a half to do that — to be there for me?"

"Yeah, I want this, Brian. I want this to be from God. I believe this message is from God." He told me this because I'd shown him notes and an outline of what I felt God had purposed for me to say in the video, and he agreed.

We arrived at the stage, and Chris told me that in 2006, he, Weylin and a bunch of friends prayed that a prophetic word would be spoken from that stage. I was blown away when I heard this because he hadn't mentioned that to me before.

"Brian, I believe this is *that* prophetic word."

At this, I started crying. I had just met this guy two weeks ago, and he had just recently come into my life because he saw me posting videos on Facebook about a revival coming to the northeastern United States. I didn't even know conclusively if I was hearing from God or not. I felt like I was. Chris went for it and reached out to me and told me that what God had laid on my heart was something God had spoken to him many years prior.

This stage was the same stage where many artists performed throughout the summer singing secular music. A lot of drinking and drugs are done in that park day in and day out. The Word of God says that we have dominion over everything because we are His children. Scripture also says that what we declare in the name of Jesus, He will do. So we walked around the stage seven times, and we declared that it was an altar for Jesus. We got on our hands and knees on the cold wet ground and prayed before we started. We prayed over the message. We prayed over the revival that would follow. We prayed for protection from any weapon coming to harm us. We prayed for the air to be cleared of any demonic forces against the will of the Father. We took our rightful position within the reign and rule of God, and that was it. That night, Chris placed his hands on my shoulder and told me, "Brian, God is going to confirm and affirm this message for you over and over again. Because you're doing this for Him, He's going to do that for you. He's going to send confirmation after confirmation."

I continued to fast the next day, Saturday, because I wanted to continue with a focused mindset when we recorded the video. I wanted to keep myself in top spiritual form and stay in direct line with the will of the

Father. Another brother in Christ, Joel Santos, had reached out to us and asked me and Eric if he could join us in the beginning stages of the revival. So he joined us in the making of the prophetic video. I asked Eric and Joel to stand out of the frame because I didn't want their lives to be in any danger. If danger came, I just wanted it to happen to me. When I told them this, they responded, "Bro, just do it. We don't care. We're going to ride with you." It was a powerful moment.

We went through a couple of still shots as Osyris, now seventeen, held the camera to see how everything would look, but otherwise it was a one-shot take. Other than taking some videos for a few seconds to make sure the camera was working and that you could hear me well, we had no redoes or retakes. The Holy Spirit just let it rip. Inspired by Jesus, I made declarations to the dealers in this area that they had seven days to cease and desist what they were doing. The Lord told me to say twenty-four hours, but I told Him that it wasn't enough time for the video to circulate and for His message to be heard. I quoted the verses from Proverbs God had given me and declared that God would take their drug money from them as the first wave of attack (Proverbs 13:11). The second wave of attack would be that anxiety and panic would overcome them (Proverbs 28:1). The third wave of attack would be the death of their lives because they were pushing death on the city of Lawrence with the distribution of fentanyl and heroin. My final declaration was that Jesus was sending His Holy Spirit to set the captives free.

At this point, I asked Eric, who knows Hebrew and Greek and who also has an amazing understanding of the Word of God, if the video had anything unbiblical or untrue. I was very concerned about declaring anything false or giving anyone anything to latch on to and nitpick. He looked at me and said, "Nope, it's good. I believe that everything you said in the video is in the Bible. Let's move on." We went on our way.

If you look at the comments section under the video on my Facebook profile[1], many people shared various articles that came out. Everything happened within seven days and in the order that Jesus told me to say it.

The day after I did the video was Resurrection Sunday. That morning, I went to my fiancée's church with her and her family. I had never heard a sermon in that church before. Of course, I had been there with Eunice but had never heard any preaching. That morning, a blind evangelist from Los Angeles spoke. As he was preaching, he said, "There will be a spiritual revival coming to this region. The Holy Spirit is going to come and clean out Lawrence. He will clear out the area." My fiancée's family tapped me to make sure I was hearing this because my mind was drifting due to all that was going on. When I heard the word "revival," I jumped up as high as I could and started screaming "Hallelujah!" as if someone lit a fire under me. I was amazed because not even twenty-four hours had passed since I had posted that video, and this evangelist was confirming it without even knowing I had posted it. I was so impacted by this. I had completely stepped out in faith, declaring Jesus was sending His Holy Spirit to set the captives free.

Early the following week, we went to Weylin's office to pray. The painting of a lion was on the wall—the one Eric had showed me on Facebook and asked me about. I hadn't previously noticed it. This time at Weylin's office, it caught my eye, so I asked him about it. Weylin told me he planned on selling it, which was the totality of our conversation about it. I left after concluding my business there.

I kept this in my spirit and felt the Holy Spirit keep telling me to check on that painting. I texted Weylin and asked him about a Scripture verse I had noticed on it. But he didn't remember it and thought it was a verse from Proverbs. I went back to his Facebook business page where I originally saw the picture because the Holy Spirit kept telling me to check it. The verse was Proverbs 13:11, which is about dishonest money dwindling away. This was the same proverb the Holy Spirit had given me when I was sweeping the floor at home. At this point, I had only known Weylin and Chris for less than three weeks. When Eric had asked me if I liked that painting, the Holy Spirit gave me Scripture for the video we recorded the previous Saturday. I became really excited at the fact that the confirmations were all over the place and was screaming for joy. I sent the picture of the lion with the verses to the other guys. We had completely stepped out in faith and had no idea that we were actually doing the will of the Father. It was amazing to see Jesus confirm these messages to keep us mentally at peace by telling us that this was His doing.

A couple of days later, Weylin called me and told me he felt he had a word from the Lord for me that God was going to confirm that this was from him. At the time of this writing, the video has been shared over seven hundred times and viewed nearly thirty thousand times. I never imagined that would happen. I know the Holy Spirit pushed and promoted that video and caused it to get that much attention. The other videos I've posted have only been viewed an average of two hundred times.

The first major drug bust reported in local media happened nine days after we posted the video. Over $500,000 in drugs were seized just like the proverb says about dishonest money dwindling away. We have the option to look at this from a spiritual perspective and see

God in the details, setting up all the stings prior to the video, or we can say that this was all planned by man and let carnal man get the glory. We choose Jesus. We say that the same way Jesus was working in and through us, He was working within law enforcement too.

From there, huge drug busts seemed to happen almost every week in Lawrence and the Merrimack Valley.[2] There were even reports of the deaths of drug lords, daytime shootings, and murders on the rise. The loss of their profits had a cascading effect; many of these drug dealers were losing large quantities of money, so the crime rate spiked. I believe those murders were the third wave of attack from the Lord. The second was that the wicked flee when no one is pursuing them (Proverbs 28:1). I don't really know for sure, and this is my opinion, but I believe that many who were caught up in this lifestyle experienced fear and anxiety as they heard about and watched FBI stings and raids happening along with kingpins and major drug dealers being arrested in large drug sweeps. I can't prove it in the natural, but I feel that many were in fear of being caught themselves just as God had me prophesy. I believe His word came true, but I don't have any documentation or media reports about the second wave. So much activity was happening in the region that it would be impossible to be a drug dealer and not feel a heightened sense of panic and anxiety.

---

1. You can watch the video and see the comments at this link: https://www.facebook.com/100010469287019/videos/vb.100010469287019/596607280698243/
2. As mentioned, there were many reports of drug busts. Here are a few headlines and links that were left as comments to the video we made, all of which were accessed on April 23rd, 2019:

    Man gets 15 years in federal prison for drug-dealing network based in Lawrence, Mass
    Source: https://www.unionleader.com/news/crime/man-gets-years-in-federal-prison-for-drug-dealing-network/article_7b14d185-e740-5a8f-9da4-d2d8754b8dd4.html

    Massive Lawrence operation feeding drugs to New Hampshire is dismantled with 45 people arrested, 60 pounds of fentanyl seized
    Source: https://www.masslive.com/news/2018/04/massive_lawrence-based_drug_op.html

    DEA Raids Several Lawrence Locations, Make Arrests Early Monday
    Source: http://valleypatriot.com/dea-raids-several-lawrence-locations-make-arrests-early-monday/

    Largest Fentanyl Bust in N.H. Traced to Lawrence Drug Ring
    https://www.nhpr.org/post/largest-fentanyl-bust-nh-traced-lawrence-drug-ring#stream/0

    9 people arrested, over $15,000 worth of drugs seized in Manchester, NH
    Source: https://whdh.com/news/9-people-arrested-over-15000-worth-of-drugs-seized-in-manchester-nh/

Fentanyl bust makes NH history
Source: https://www.eagletribune.com/news/new_hampshire/fentanyl-bust-makes-nh-history/article_c6efc8c2-4967-11e8-895b-e3c7507eddaf.html

There are many more I could link to, but you get the idea.

THE LION AND THE EAGLE

AFTER THIS, I randomly started hearing sermons about eagles and lions everywhere. For example, I came across sermons on YouTube and listened to them. I would just click on it, and a preacher would be breaking down how God identifies with the lion and how the lion is the king of the land. He would talk about how God identifies with the eagle, which is the king of the air, and share other inspirational and informative material. I learned so much after publishing the video until the end of the year.

In Haverhill, the city where I live at the time of this writing, there was a report about a kid who died, and I was asked to speak at a peace rally. I said yes because ever since I reconciled with the Lord, I made a deal with Him that I'd say yes to whatever someone asked of me, especially if His people were asking for any type of assistance. I wanted to serve God, my community, and anyone around me to the best of my ability. Even if they want me to come and cut their lawn with a pair of scissors, I would still have said yes. Thankfully, I'm rarely taken advantage of in this way, but I digress. I went to speak at this rally and didn't realize until later that the local newspaper, *The Eagle Tribune*, was there.

Key word: eagle.

After the event, we went to another building for some refreshments, and on my way outside, a news reporter approached me, asking my name. I told him, and he told me that what I said during the speech at the *Stop the Violence Peace Rally* was powerful. This blessed me because all I did was repeat God's Word without sharing my own thoughts. I wasn't yelling or being super emotional like I tend to be when I preach or speak publicly. I was calm and simply spoke the love of Jesus over the community.

As I was talking with this reporter, I felt the Holy Spirit say to me, "Now's the time to plug your business ventures during this conversation." The reporter asked me if I was a pastor, and I told him no but that I was a student in preparation to become a pastor. During this brief conversation, I mentioned that I was an inventor, which seemed to interest him even further.

"An inventor? What did you invent?"

"A few things," I said, as I started to tell him about CathWear.

"CathWear? Underwear? What do you mean? Like you own the patent?" he asked.

"Yeah, I'm also a nurse."

"You're a nurse?"

"Yeah. I also have my degree in radiology from Northern Essex Community College." The school was right down the street.

"Wait a minute! Do you have a business card?" he asked. I did, so I pulled one out and gave it to him. "I want to talk to you. I want to digest this. I need to sit down with you and learn more about who you are and more about this invention. My family grew up in the mills in the textile industry, and if you're building something that will go back into these mills so that they open back up, I want to be a part of that."

I talked to him some more that day and went to be interviewed at *The Eagle Tribune*. He ended up writing a fairly long article on CathWear, my first of many inventions.

When I walked into their offices, he asked me where I'd like to do the photos. I didn't know where to set up, so I asked him to pick a spot since this was his territory. He suggested that I walk around the building and find a place. It was after business hours, so I began walking around. I picked a spot inside *The Eagle Tribune*. I had no idea that the background of the wall was under an enormous eagle's wing. The design was an abstract silhouette, a huge open space. When I sent the picture to one of my friends, he screamed, "Brian, the eagle!"

By the end of the year, I used that image as my background picture on Facebook. When 2018 started, I wanted to have those two pictures of the eagle and the lion on my Facebook profile. I asked the Lord to share about this eagle and the lion with me. If you look up the archived article that was in *The Eagle Tribune*, you'll see that I constantly mention God whenever I talk about CathWear.

At the end, the interviewer called me on the phone to ask me a question: "Why do you want to be a preacher?"

I was a little bit stunned, and I froze, not because I couldn't answer him or because I didn't know. I'd just never been asked that before. I felt the Holy Spirit impress on me to tell him that I wanted to spread God's truth. I didn't say *the* truth, because the truth is subjective. I wanted to say God's truth because it's objective; it's undeniable.

That visit to *The Eagle Tribune* is just one more example of many of seeing eagles everywhere. I went to

Atlanta at the end of 2018 to a major event to showcase CathWear. I didn't realize we were across the street from the Atlanta Falcons stadium. As we drove around the stadium, I noticed a huge falcon (or eagle) and took a picture with it right behind me. This was significant to me because this event was an enormous success, and the Lord opened many more business avenues for us at this trade show. The path to grow CathWear has been effortless, which is how I know that this project is empowered by Jesus who is God.

#GODMANCE

AFTER I RECORDED the video in the park the Holy Spirit made through us, I was considered radical and unbiblical. I can certainly see how people would have this perception of me since I had a drastic change in my life. If I were them, I would think the same: that Brian was just in it for self gain. In the local body of Christ, few seemed to want to associate with me after the video was posted online and spread. It was a very powerful show of the Lord's ability to move in the hearts of men. His Word was clearly spoken, and it will never return void. (See Isaiah 55:11.) People were saying that the video was too out there and that I had made a fool of myself. I certainly didn't feel that way nor have I ever had the urge or been convicted to delete the video. The peace of the Lord was on me during this time. Where the Spirit of the Lord is there is freedom (2 Corinthians 3:17). I went to the bodega and ordered breakfast right after I filmed it. Again, because I had been fasting with no food or water for over 24 hours to make sure I was as close to my spiritual form within Christ as I could be. I was hungry!

I heard the chatter. To be honest with you, I sometimes struggle with anxiety, so it was challenging to resist it and not let it get to me, but I kept repeating Scripture toward the devil who was making every effort to harass me. I know the Lord was giving me the victory over my anxiety. After that prayer encounter in my house the Thursday before recording it, I never once felt anxiety about it again. The video had hundreds of comments and was shared by hundreds of pastors all over the Northeast and from as far away as Florida. One misinformed individual accused the video of being new age garbage and called it a metaphysical theological cult. I had no idea what he meant. Other than that, not one person has complained to date. I did it for the Lord, and it was up to Him to fight my battles regarding the video. It was my job to be obedient.

THE HEROIN EPIDEMIC CONTINUED

In this region there is a lot of disconnectedness within the local Body of Christ. It is mainly very territorial and many members do not associate with believers from other churches. If there's an event at another fellowship then only the members of that church attend, and it's not very inviting. If you invite other churches to your own events they don't come or if they do they don't post any pictures to social media while there, as if it's some secret.

A local church organizes a men's conference around June every year. The event is held two hours up north in New Hampshire. I attended many of these conferences when I was a member of this church and had reconciled my relationship with Christ. After 2 years, I left this church and then having posted the prophetic video, I felt unsure of my relationship with the members and pastors there. I admit that I'm not sure whether that was on my own or whether the Lord had impressed it on me. I simply had a sense that this pastor did not like the video at all because they don't believe in the gifts of the Holy Spirit still operating today. I really wanted to go to their men's conference and just fellowship all of us together. Many of the churches here struggle with division and keep to themselves, and I feel God has placed it in my heart to be a part of the solution and not contribute to the problem. I believe that's why you see so many churches within such a short distance of each other in Lawrence. It's very healthy to have multi-church gatherings. I wanted to worship the Lord Jesus with everyone on a larger scale because more than a thousand men attend each year.

The Holy Spirit had me reach out to this pastor shortly after I had made the video, so I sent him a direct message a couple of months before the conference. I hadn't talked to him since I had left his church. I had just gotten on social media, particularly Facebook, two years prior to writing this book shortly after I had reconciled my relationship with God. I told this man that I had been thinking about going to the event and felt in my spirit that I needed to reach out to him directly and find out if that was okay. Even before he replied to my text, I discerned what he would say. I understand his concern for his church and he has an obligation to protect his church and its members from anything which seems spiritually abnormal to him. His response was beyond what I anticipated or expected and not in a good way. He wrote a short novel in his response! Some of the words were in all caps, and he expressed that he had no idea what I meant about the churches not being unified. He felt that they were more unified than ever and suggested that maybe the division and walls I was referring to were all in my heart and that maybe I needed to examine myself. He told me that he was now conducting seminars with Pentecostals, Baptists, and evangelicals and opening new churches everywhere. He indicated that church planting was at an all-time high in New England. He also said that if I wanted to come that I should realize that they don't speak in tongues or lay hands on people. He even made sure to put these particular comments in all caps and along with another point he made about not doing anything supposedly outside of biblical guidelines. He said that they agree on the majors but leave the minors alone.

The message was a hard pill to swallow, to say the least, because he was clearly telling me not to attend. As I continued reading, I sensed that he was worried that I wanted to come and leverage a position for myself as an up and coming Christian leader in the area. He said these exact words. "If you're coming to gain leverage or push an agenda to boost yourself up, then maybe this isn't for you." Many of the churches in New England focus on the numbers within the church walls and I believe the Bible says to focus on repentance and salvation. I know it's important to keep the focus on the Lord and not keep the focus on any man, so I certainly agree with his thought process to a certain extent.

The response on Messenger went on and on, but

these were a few of the highlights. I got a sense of "if we see anything funny, you're going to be asked to leave." He told me that a person once went to his men's conference who was laying hands on people and praying healing over their ailments. That man was asked to stop. But this person kept on laying hands on people who needed prayer despite their request. So he was asked to leave and never attend unless he would stop operating in his spiritual gifts. I was totally shocked as I repeatedly read his response.

All I could say was "wow" out loud after reading his message. When I had finished, anxiety kicked in hard. I responded to this pastor in love as best I could, but the line was drawn in the sand. Any affiliation I had with this church came to a permanent end that night. It didn't require a lot of godly discernment to realize I probably shouldn't attend! So when June came around, I didn't go.

I kept asking the Holy Spirit about one comment he had made. He said, "Churches are more unified than ever before." He was conducting seminars to "teach a bunch of different congregations how to church plant." My question for the Holy Spirit then was, "If the churches are more unified than ever before, then why are we in the middle of a heroin epidemic?" I've repeatedly heard that the condition of the community is the condition of the churches. One day, the Lord spoke into my spirit and clearly said, "Church planting is not a sign of revival and unity among the churches. The repentance of man is." At this revelation, I just cracked a big smile. It's amazing how living and active the Holy Spirit is for us believers today.

In the beginning of 2018, I had a conversation with Eric Diaz, and we talked about how cool it would be to hold a men's conference. I believe this was the time the Lord had ordained to implement this idea. In the meantime, I got mad at the Lord immediately after I had the previously mentioned conversation with the pastor. I yelled at God and asked Him if I had done His will, then why was I a black sheep within the body of Christ? I asked Him why I was viewed as a lunatic.

"Why am I viewed as radical and unbiblical?" I yelled at Him. I didn't understand it. "Lord, what are you going to do about what's happening to this community? I want a revival; that's what I want! That's what this is all about!" I cried out. "I want people to know who you are. What are you going to do?"

He replied, "What am I going to do? I already made my move on the cross. My job is finished. What are *you* going to do?"

I said, "Nobody wants to work with me!"

"I am the one that puts kings in place and who takes

them down. I am the one who made (the local pastor). Whatever you are looking for from him, I am the one who can provide it for you!" He answered. God then went on to ask me, *"What do you want, Brian?"*

I replied, "I want to do a men's conference."

"So just make the move and start one, and I'll back it up!" I was so humbled at His words. I just started laughing and thought, *"Okay, that's all you had to say."*

During that same season, my fiancée, Eunice, repeatedly pointed out a verse to me, but I wasn't paying attention. Second Chronicles 16:9 says, "For the eyes of the Lord run to and fro throughout the whole earth, to show Himself strong on behalf of those whose heart is loyal to Him." She kept telling me, "Brian, that's your verse." You see, this is just another example of how the Word of God is alive. It will apply at the exact moment needed to implement the Lord's will. The verse didn't make sense at first. But after that conversation with God, I strongly felt that I needed to go look up that verse again, and of course, it hit me between the eyes. I told the Lord, "Okay, you've spoken. Your Word says that you're looking for people to show your power to. Well, I'm taking this, and I'm going to do something with it. Just back me up."

"Okay," He replied.

The name #GODMANCE had popped into my

mind by the power of the Holy Spirit. It was a mix of bromance and a loving relationship with God. I didn't come up with this original word. I Googled it and other results showed up, but I had never heard this word previously. The idea behind it was having a bromance with my friend Eric, which people used to tell us all the time. If close male friends can have a bromance, then why don't we have a #GODMANCE that's even stronger? The hashtag in front of it updated the word so that it could be used across social media platforms.

We started putting the vision together, but I hadn't yet mentioned the name of this conference to him. Around this time, his wife had a miscarriage which was very difficult for Eric and his family. As a result, this project was put on the back burner for a while. We had declared spiritual revival back in March before I had started making all these Facebook videos based on Job 22:28, "You will also declare a thing, and it will be established for you; so light will shine on your ways."

But the #GODMANCE conference planning was placed on hold. Around the same time, I met Les Brinkley, who lives in Florida, through the Marco Polo app, a social media group app. Les randomly looked through my old videos and saw one that Eric and I made focusing on Job 22:28 earlier in March. Eric was in the group chat as well but dropped out a short time later. Les called me up out of the blue and told me, "You and Eric have a mandate for that area" This reaffirmed our calling to that region. He continued, "You guys *have* to continue that revival." Les had two teenage sons who had died, and so he told us, "The devil is trying to derail Eric like he tried to derail me. Brian, if you talk to Eric, show him this video and tell him that I told him he needs to man up. He needs to pick up his sword, and you guys need to continue with this revival!"

Nobody knew that the word #GODMANCE was circulating in my head except God. During this phone call, Les spoke life into me, telling me that a revival was coming to our region and that God was going to do it through Eric and me. Les repeated that we needed to obey God's mandate over our lives so that we could see revival in our region. Then he said something that really caught my attention. "You and Eric, man, you have like this bromance. You guys love God, so it's really like a GODMANCE."

"What?" I replied, wondering if my ears were playing tricks on me.

"You guys have like a GODMANCE." He repeated himself.

And right then, *boom*! On that spot, at that second, I knew the Holy Spirit had confirmed the message and word about the men's conference. From there on, we put the whole conference together. The fact that the word God had given me came out of the mouth of this guy from Florida whom I had never met before was completely the Lord showing me that the same Holy Spirit dwelling in me was also living in Les Brinkley. I started yelling in excitement during this conversation with Les.

The conference was to be held the second week of August. Two weeks before that, the Holy Spirit told me as I was driving on Route 28 in New Hampshire, "Don't ever take #GODMANCE out of the Merrimack Valley. Promise me you that you will leave it there, no matter what. I want it to stay right there."

To this I responded, "I promise."

As I mentioned earlier, President Trump talked about the heroin epidemic here in this area. The Holy Spirit told me, "The stage has been set." The situation had been made clear to me so that God's power would be made strong and shown through us. In a similar way, God allowed Pharaoh's heart to become hard so that He would make His power known through him. I believe the heroin epidemic had become that bad so that it would reach a tipping point. God could then start the revival and receive the glory for ending that epidemic instead of man or local law enforcement. I feel that this is precisely why God told me to never take the #GOD-

MANCE conference from the Merrimack Valley. Most men's retreats take the men out of the homes and region, which can certainly have benefits. Some men can't attend these conferences because they can't take off time from work or due to other obligations. The purpose of #GODMANCE was to have a local gathering of men in an area where spiritual warfare was very active due to the condition of the community. It was a free event for anyone to attend. This gathering was for men from different churches to worship the Lord our God under one roof. We decided to conduct it in the middle of the day so that people could attend if they were running errands or what not.

If men have to travel to far-away conferences, they return tired from the long weekend and aren't as energetic after fellowshipping with other believers. The men's conference that I chose not to attend has a lot of hype and emotion, but little conviction in the message. Most men just returned with little change. You could tell this by what was said after the conference and the social media posts during and after the conference. Not much spiritual fruit was displayed when the men went home. Our community remained the same: broken.

#GODMANCE would allow for the men to be charged up with the love of Jesus and to then quickly pour His love into their wives, children, and the community. This conference would focus on worship and the Word. We wouldn't be whipping around a football or cooking burgers. We wanted to create an atmosphere where the Holy Spirit could move on the hearts of men to inspire us to turn our lives back to the presence of the Father.

The men who attended commented about how impacting and powerful it was. Many lives were touched with numerous testimonies of people reconciling their relationship with the Lord. We plan to continue this conference every year in the same region, and we will bombard the region with other conferences, and #GODMANCE will be just one of them. The hope for this conference is to hold it in a different church in the Merrimack Valley every year to create a bond and unity within the body of Christ and to generate a new epidemic. I stepped out in obedience for the Lord, and He backed up my faith like He told me He would.

After the conference, we conducted water baptisms. Five people were baptized in water, and seven people gave their lives to Christ. Almost two hundred men showed up for this amazing move of God on this region. All glory be to God for the results of this event.

When I was still far from God, my mom came to my house and told me I would be a preacher. I would laugh and blow smoke in her face. She would tell me, "It doesn't matter what you do, Brian. God is going to turn you into a preacher. Before I die, I will hear you preach the Word of God!" This was so far from my mind that I didn't even pay attention. My mother has now watched me preach quite a few times as of this writing. The apostle Paul talks about this when he mentions Lois, Timothy's grandmother, and his mother Eunice who used to speak life into Timothy and give him encouraging words (see 2 Timothy 1:6). I never realized I was listening to a prophecy spoken over my life by my mother. It's amazing to watch it all play out and the joy on my mother's face when she sees me working diligently for the Lord.

EVANGELISM EXPLOSION

IN APRIL 2018, I went on a mission trip, and our pastor used the term "evangelism explosion" while we were working on a building at Teen Challenge damaged by Hurricane Maria in Bayamon, Puerto Rico. Pastor Rick Amendola was speaking to someone else when I overheard him say this. The words resonated with me, and later God would involve me in organizing an event with this name in the area. As of the writing of this book, I am scheduled to present the initial installment of this training.

I love talking to people about the goodness of the Lord our God. It brings life to my soul and fills every part of my being.

On one occasion, early in my reconciliation with the Lord, my youngest son was sick. I went to the pharmacy to buy some over-the-counter medicine, and my eyes were drawn to a bookshelf there. A book titled *The Gifts and Ministries of the Holy Spirit* covered in dust was on the bottom shelf. I couldn't look away from it. I picked it up and wiped off the dust and purchased it. Toward the end of the book, I found this quote. "Do you feel a call to evangelism? Then go out into your own neighborhood, to your neighbors and friends, and get somebody saved. Go across town to someone you have never seen before and see if you can lead him or her to Jesus."[1]

After I finished the book, I started approaching people, albeit awkwardly, and told them something as simple as "Jesus loves you." Little by little and by God's grace and instruction, I became better at evangelism to the point where it's really led by the Holy Spirit now. Second Corinthians 5:20 says, "Now then, we are ambassadors for Christ, as though God were pleading through us: we implore you on Christ's behalf, be reconciled to God."

I've seen people start crying when I talk to them about Jesus, my testimony and the goodness of the Lord. He came into my life and changed it to be completely effective for Him. This is proof of the power of the blood of Christ and what was done at the cross at Calvary. I know I've been called as an evangelist, which has been spoken over my life by God as well.

Over fifteen years ago, someone I'd never met or even seen before came up to me at a church gathering and asked me if I was an evangelist. At the time, I didn't even know what an evangelist was or what the word meant. He continued, "You're an evangelist. I've seen you before. I've seen you in a stadium preaching to an audience of ten thousand people. God used you to bring people to Him. You're an evangelist!" I never saw that guy again, but I ended up looking up the word evangelist when I got home. After I learned what an evangelist was, I thought, *Okay, whatever*, since this was many years before I reconciled with God, and I didn't have a clue as to who He was. I have not yet seen the complete fulfillment of this prophecy. But I think God will fulfill His word, and I share that here as a public record and for accountability before it happens. All these years later, I'm about to be used by God to unleash evangelism explosion conferences along with #GODMANCE in a part of the country that has been declared to have a heroin epidemic by the president of the United States. God is amazing! The reason I'm starting this in our part of the country is because "I know that my Redeemer lives, and He shall stand at last on the earth" (Job 19:25). I know Jesus is alive!

When I heard our pastor utter those words "evangelism explosion," I researched the term on Google. I jumped at the nearest opportunity and headed to Arkansas for a two-day seminar on how to effectively evangelize. I had a misconception of what spreading the gospel of Jesus Christ or evangelism was. Evangelism Explosion, founded by Dr. James Kennedy, is a systematic and proven process to help you share your faith with complete strangers. It helps build relationships and discover when people are open to spiritual conversations. It's a great tool to learn how to talk about the spiritual realm. I will be using the skills I've learned in Evangelism Explosion in ministry for the rest of my life.

Evangelism Explosion allows you to establish a renewed vision and enthusiasm for personal witnessing. The *Share Your Faith Seminar* outlines five easy steps so that you can remember it.[2] As you are around friends and family, you can help them discover the next steps in their spiritual journey. When you are a witness of the gospel, you need to remove fear and gain confidence.

I just want to grow and work everything God gives me as the parable of the talents in Matthew 25:14–30 describes. That's one of the aspects of my addictive personality. I used to think that addictive personality was just a cliché, but I looked up the term when I was still bound to drugs. People with an addictive personality focus on something and can't rest or stop until they've achieved or obtained it.

I treat the everlasting Word of God in this manner now; I got a hold of it, and the Lord has just unlocked my brain. I want it! I pray and dive into the written Word every single day, and at least four days of the week, for sixty to ninety minutes. When I haven't prayed or spent time in the Word of God in a few days, I feel it. I can also see my addictive personality being used by God to bring people to Him. This is how He turns all things into a positive. I asked the trainer in Arkansas why Evangelism Explosion wasn't in the Northeast. He responded, "New England is the coldest place in the country. We haven't been able to start a training center up there, and it will take someone with a lot of passion and endurance to implement it and see it progress." I can clearly see why we're in the early stages of a major revival here. The spiritual activity is so thick at the time of writing this book, which is very hard to explain unless you're experiencing it. I've never seen the Holy Spirit move in the way he's moving right now.

If the Lord allows, I plan on making the Evangelism Explosion at New Life Christian Church the biggest, best, and most-effective training center the earth has ever seen. Revival started in New England, and I believe the revival happening right now will last until the second coming of Christ.

There's so much power in Scripture. It's unbelievable how the Holy Spirit still speaks to us today. It amazes me how such value has been in that written Word for thousands of years, waiting to be extrapolated by those of us who want it, but many don't even bother. Everything in the Bible is being played out right before our very eyes, and nobody is paying attention to it. I include myself at one time in my life.

---

1. Lester Sumrall, *The Gifts and Ministries of the Holy Spirit* (Pennsylvania: Whitaker House, 1982) 261.
2. "Share Your Faith," *Evangelism Explosion International*, accessed April 9, 2019, https://evangelismexplosion.org/ministries/share-your-faith.

REDEMPTION: CONCLUDING THOUGHTS

THE WORD of God says in John 10:10 that "The thief does not come except to steal, and to kill, and to destroy. I have come that they may have life, and that they may have it more abundantly." My life is a living testimony to this truth, but probably especially so in my new marriage. An important part of the journey on my way back to Christ was the implosion of my first marriage, so I don't want to leave the readers hanging if they wondered about some comments and references I've made as to if I've remarried. The answer to that is heck, yes!

The Lord Jesus is a God of restoration. He has the ability to create something from nothing, which is where my reconciliation started: from the bottom. I don't want to end this book and neglect to glorify God for restoring what the locusts have eaten (Joel 2:25) in *every* area of my life. But before I get to that, I want to tell you what happened while I was working on this manuscript.

One morning, I was in prayer, and I asked God to do something special for me that day. It didn't matter what it was in particular, even if it was just revelatory insight. Whatever it was, good or bad, I'd accept as His will in my life.

Since I'm a visiting nurse, I spend much of my time driving around, seeing my patients. On this particular day, I had no reason to go to my office, but I felt a nudge to drive there anyway since I hadn't been in a while. When I entered, I saw a letter from Lawrence High School with my name on it, sitting right on top of my desk. I kept checking the date over and over because I was surprised to see this letter from one of my old principals, part of the alumni association who used to work with my dad.

I opened it to find an invitation to speak at the school. They had been watching me and reading my articles in the newspaper and listening to my interviews on the local radio. The letter said they were inspired and wanted me to speak to the students. They want me to speak at the school as a keynote speaker and they're naming a scholarship after me.

I believe this was total vindication, the kind of vindication that is soaked in God's favor and that can only come from His throne. I previously mentioned that my family was completely shamed after what had happened to my dad, and now God was using this to bring glory to His name.

At that time, my family was severed and never repaired. I now see God was moving and doing something powerful through this event. I include it here at the end of this book as this event is scheduled for May 2019, shortly after this book is due to be released. I'm honored just to have been invited.

You see, I didn't get to attend my graduation ceremony. A few guys and I were caught with alcohol and drugs on our senior trip to Disneyland and were expelled from school. I had to attend summer school that year to receive my diploma, but I didn't get to walk in a cap and gown with my peers. The friends I was expelled with went to the graduation ceremony to see our friends graduate, but when we arrived, we were told that we would not be allowed to attend the ceremony.

That was a very dark time in my life, during the same season when my father dealt with all the legal issues prior to heading to prison. That whole period of my life hurt me a lot, but I put most of the events about graduation out of my mind until I received the letter that day. Now the Lord is bringing me back to a place that brought me so much shame, embarrassment, and pain as the keynote speaker to give a motivational speech.

In all my posts on social media and whenever I have a speaking engagement, I try to make sure the first word I write or the first idea I convey is Jesus. I want Him to be preeminent in all I say and do so that He goes first and covers me. Ephesians 1:7 says, *"In Him we have redemption through His blood, the forgiveness of sins, according to the riches of His grace."* I live and breathe to make as many people as I come across aware of the reality of His redemptive goodness.

Now I will have the platform at my old high school and speak to about six hundred people. I will highlight the love of God and the sacrifice of Jesus Christ and weave these naturally into my speech. I'm not planning on hitting religious themes hard in my speech, but it's impossible to share my story and leave out why I'm transformed: the blood of Jesus. I'm going to make sure they know that I have done everything I've done since they last saw me through the grace of God.

Glory be to God!

So to get back to remarriage: God has restored that part of my life and redeemed it in ways above and beyond anything I could ever have imagined. I don't want to go into too much detail about my marriage and how I met Eunice other than to say that the devil fails because he's a loser and a punk.

A big part of my journey was how my marriage and family were destroyed by a combination of consequences for my actions and onslaught from the enemy who seeks to steal, kill, and destroy. I didn't want to leave out that detail of my life. I want to make sure you know that God has restored me in all the areas of my life that I talked about in this book.

For a while, after committing my life to Christ, I kept randomly dating, trying to fill this void in my life. But after five months of sobriety, in early 2016, I finally told my mom and my pastor that I was going to turn this nightmare into a positive outcome to bring glory to God. I never thought that the Lord would bring someone into my life that I had gone to Lawrence High School with twenty-five years earlier.

This sounds silly to admit now, but I sent a lot of friend requests to women on Facebook, which I have obviously stopped doing since I met Eunice. I looked at it like a free dating website and like shooting fish in a barrel, until one day, on the "people you may know" section of Facebook, I saw her profile. I hit the button to send a friend request and started seeing her posts in my newsfeed.

I had no idea who she was and kept seeing her post

about spiritual topics. One day, I decided to supposedly stalk her on Facebook, so I checked out her profile details and other pictures more closely. To make a long story short, I asked her brother if she was dating anyone and what he thought about me asking her out. He suggested that we pray about it, and we both got down on our knees in our respective homes. I'll never forget that prayer.

Eunice is the only woman (or person) I asked God for permission to meet.

She comes from the same background that I do of drugs, alcohol, and cigarettes, and God saved her too. She's free from that lifestyle as well and really loves the Lord. We are now very happily married, and she's also going to Bible school with me. She's awesome.

God gave me exactly what I had asked for in a wife and much more. For that, I am eternally grateful.

In closing, I realize some people might think a few years in the Lord is too soon to write a biographical book like this, but I disagree. I want to share my testimony so Jesus can set as many captives free through my life story and transformation. I know this message and my story will do exactly that. This book can reach and touch people I can't physically get to.

Someone once told me, "Brian, you're just on fire because you're a new Christian. That will wear off in time." That's one of the dumbest things that people can say, especially to a recent convert. I pray that person's heart becomes reignited because I don't want to ever become cold and complacent like that.

I just don't want to stop. I'm not going to stop. I won't quit surrendering my life to Christ over and over again and killing the old me. I want people to know what I know and what God taught me because it really set me free! It set me free from the desires of this world. I no longer chase finances, material possessions, or women. These are all being given to me.

The article in *The Eagle Tribune* gave us free advertising for CathWear. As of yet, I haven't spent one single dime on advertising or marketing for the company. I made it on the magazine cover at one of the colleges I graduated from. At the time of this writing, I'm going to be on the cover of a second magazine from another college I attended. And like I mentioned, I'm scheduled to be the keynote speaker for an assembly at my old high school.

All of it is free marketing and God promoting what He's doing in and through me. I'm not trying to make anything happen on my own or for my own glory.

It's all *Him*.

It's all God.

The devil is the father of lies. He was a murderer

from the beginning and does not stand in truth because there is no truth in him. When he speaks a lie, he speaks from his own resources, for he is a liar and the father of it (John 8:44). He is the accuser of the brethren. He disguises himself as an angel of light, so his voice is very deceptive. The devil lied to me and to all of humanity. He lied to me about who I really was, and I unknowingly partnered with him to destroy my life through my poor decision-making. At that point, I didn't know that we are heirs to the kingdom of heaven because of the blood sacrifice from the Father through Jesus on the cross. It's truly special to think that heaven is real, and we now have access to the most holy place because of Jesus. We are now the children and people of God. My life outside of Jesus is useless, but my life under His righteousness gives me power to do the Lord's will.

Satan cannot return to heaven because he tried to be like God, so he was kicked out of the reign and rule of God. Now he tries to twist everything beautiful about God's creation in order to keep us out of heaven as well. He can only distort and warp the things of God because the devil doesn't have the ability to create. He is much more limited than we think. But we have intelligence through the Holy Spirit that supersedes anything the forces of darkness can come up with. The devil is very smart, but greater is He who is living in me than he who is in the world (1 John 4:4).

He wants us to chase everything and anything just so that we don't chase God. I'm not as driven to succeed here on earth now that I know we live forever in eternity with Jesus. I don't feel the rush to succeed according to man's standards. All I want to do is love God with all my heart, mind, soul, and strength and love my neighbor as myself (Mark 12:30–31). I find so much joy in doing what Matthew 6:33 says, which is to "seek first the kingdom of God and His righteousness, and all these things will be added to you." There is a joy in working for Jesus that I can't explain. It is absolutely amazing to be in the presence of God. The way I feel now is the way I thought I felt when I used alcohol and cocaine.

I'm successful through the victory of Jesus on the cross at Calvary. The blood of Jesus gives us the ultimate access to a royal priesthood. I don't fear death because those in Christ Jesus will not face any death.. I'm here to advance the kingdom of God and then to move on into the next realm ... heaven!

In closing, I want to end this book with the psalmist's words. *"Let the redeemed of the Lord say so, whom He has redeemed from the hand of the enemy"* (Psalm 107:2).

ABOUT THE AUTHOR

Brian Mohika is a registered nurse with multiple science degrees and owns several medical patents on inventions, and is the CEO of a medical device company called CathWear. Brian has continued his education by attending ministry leadership school to be an ordained pastor to preach the Gospel as a traveling evangelist. Brian is now the Men's Ministry Leader at New Life Christian and he's also a very active member within the community.

He has co-founded numerous annual conferences in the Merrimack Valley with the intention to spark revival in the immediate area. Brian's heart is to lend his powerful voice to spread the Gospel of Jesus Chris through public speaking engagements in the hopes of enlightening others to the truth about eternity.

www.ingramcontent.com/pod-product-compliance
Lightning Source LLC
Chambersburg PA
CBHW060533080526
44586CB00012B/715